Original title:
After We Parted

Copyright © 2024 Swan Charm
All rights reserved.

Author: Kaido Väinamäe
ISBN HARDBACK: 978-9916-89-781-2
ISBN PAPERBACK: 978-9916-89-782-9
ISBN EBOOK: 978-9916-89-783-6

The Abyss Between Our Souls

In shadows deep where silence cries,
Two spirits fight beneath the skies.
A chasm wide, yet whispers gleam,
Faith flickers softly, a fragile dream.

Each prayer ascends like smoke entwined,
With hopes that wane, yet must be blind.
For in the void, the heart must yearn,
And in the silence, lessons learn.

Wandering Through the Wasteland of Faith

A barren land stretches far and wide,
Where echoes of the faithful bide.
The footsteps faint on cracked and dry,
In search of truth, beneath the sky.

Yet in the dust, a seed may find,
A chance to bloom, the heart aligned.
Hope scattered like grains of sand,
In stillness grows a guiding hand.

Anointed by Absence

In every loss, a grief so pure,
Anointed souls learn to endure.
The sacred space where silence dwells,
In absence, there the spirit swells.

From emptiness, the heart can sing,
A melody the shadows bring.
Through voids we find the light of grace,
In every tear, a soft embrace.

The Gospel of What Once Was

In remnants of a time gone by,
We seek the truth that will not die.
The whispers of the ancient lore,
Guide us to a sacred shore.

The stories carried in the night,
Illuminate the dark with light.
In memories, our faith is spun,
The gospel speaks of all we've won.

The Choir of Forgotten Echoes

In shadows deep, their voices rise,
A chorus lost beneath the skies.
Whispers of saints, in silence weave,
The tales of dreams that none believe.

In twilight's grasp, the echoes play,
Remnants of hope in disarray.
Each note a tear, each breath a prayer,
For souls that wander, unaware.

They sing of grace and love once pure,
Of promises that fate won't secure.
With every sound, the past unfolds,
In melodies that time beholds.

Yet as the night begins to fade,
Their symphony, in silence laid.
A gentle hush, a sacred space,
Where lost and found embrace with grace.

In memory's light, they shall remain,
The choir sings through joy and pain.
With every echo, hearts shall know,
The strength within the depths of woe.

Eulogies of the Everlasting

In fields of light, where shadows part,
The eulogies of love depart.
With whispered words of ancient lore,
They honor lives that are no more.

Each tear a testament to grace,
A journey lost in time and space.
Through valleys dark, the spirits roam,
In search of peace, a final home.

The heartbeats echo, soft and low,
In every breeze, the stories flow.
With gentle hands, they touch the ground,
In sacred soil, their hopes are found.

Through sacred rites, the past ignites,
The flame of faith, through endless nights.
Each sigh a prayer, each breath a song,
In unity, where all belong.

Together now, we stand and share,
The love that lingers in the air.
In the embrace of the divine,
Eulogies flow, with hearts entwined.

In the Temple of Solitary Grief

Within these walls of silent tears,
I gather hope, confront my fears.
The whispers haunt, yet softly call,
In this great temple where shadows fall.

Each candle burns for love once lost,
A glimmer bright, despite the cost.
With every flicker, memories rise,
As faith endures through darkened skies.

In solitude, I kneel and pray,
For peace to guide my weary way.
These stones, they hold each aching sigh,
A testament to those who cry.

Yet in the pain, a strength unfolds,
In sacred space, the heart beholds.
Through hollow breaths, the spirit weaves,
A tapestry that never leaves.

From grief's embrace, new light may soar,
In this temple, I find my core.
With every prayer, I rise anew,
In solitude, I learn what's true.

Threads of Fate and Fractured Love

Along the loom, our fates entwine,
In patterns wrought from love divine.
Yet threads unravel, hearts take flight,
In fractured dreams that haunt the night.

Each stitch a promise, bold and bright,
Yet shadows linger, shrouded light.
In tangled webs, the stories bleed,
Of whispered vows and silent need.

The tapestry reflects our pain,
In every loss, we learn to gain.
Through gossamer, our truths reveal,
The love we felt, the wounds we heal.

Yet hope persists, a golden thread,
In every heart where love has bled.
Through trials faced, together strong,
In fractured love, we find our song.

So weave with care, and hold it tight,
Through shadows deep, we seek the light.
In threads of fate, our spirits soar,
A love that echoes evermore.

In the Silence of the Divine

In the hush of night we find,
A whisper from the unseen hand.
Heaven's grace in shadows bind,
With faith, we walk on sacred land.

Beneath the stars, we kneel in prayer,
Voices soft, like tender sighs.
The love of God is everywhere,
In silence, the spirit flies.

Moments still, where time stands still,
Echoes of eternity call.
Hearts aligned with holy will,
In God's embrace, we are all.

With each breath, we feel the light,
Guiding us through darkest days.
In the silence, pure and bright,
We find our path, we find our ways.

Let our hearts be filled with grace,
As we walk this sacred line.
In the silence, we embrace,
The love that's wholly divine.

A Mass for the Unforgotten

Gathered here in sacred space,
We honor those who've passed away.
With heavy heart, yet full of grace,
We lift their names in prayer today.

Candles flicker, shadows dance,
Each flame a soul that shines so bright.
In our hearts, their love will prance,
As we remember them tonight.

Voices rise, a gentle hymn,
For the ones who walked before.
Their spirits soar, on faith we brim,
In our hearts, they live forevermore.

Through the tears, a joyful smile,
We celebrate the life they led.
In our memories, they'll stay awhile,
Living on, though their bodies fled.

In this mass, we stand as one,
Bound by love, a thread so fine.
Their journey ends, but not begun,
In every heart, their light will shine.

Rites of Passage and Remembrance

In every life, we mark the change,
As seasons shift and moments blend.
Through trials vast, the heart must range,
In every ending, love transcends.

Gathered round, we share the tales,
Of journeys taken, paths well-trod.
With laughter sweet, as memory sails,
We celebrate the gift of God.

In sacred rites, we bind the past,
In whispered words, their essence stays.
For those we love, their bonds are cast,
In every tear, a lifetime plays.

With gratitude, we raise our voice,
For every life that shaped our own.
In their spirit, we rejoice,
For in our hearts, they've brightly shone.

Through every passage, we embrace,
The threads of time that never break.
In remembrance, we find our place,
In love's sweet echo, we awake.

Fading Halos

In the twilight of sacred grace,
Whispers linger, a soft embrace.
Angels weep for days slipped by,
Fading halos, lost in the sky.

Shadows dance in the hollow night,
Faith, a beacon, dimmed its light.
Hope's last breath, a silent prayer,
Fading halos, hearts laid bare.

Each tear a testament, each sigh,
Fading echoes, a mournful cry.
Yet in the dark, a spark may gleam,
Fading halos, a fragmented dream.

Hold the love, through darkest hours,
In forsaken fields, grace still flowers.
For while the light may slowly wane,
Fading halos, love will remain.

So seek the warmth in the chill of dawn,
For the spirit lives where hope is drawn.
A miracle bound by thread so fine,
Fading halos, eternally shine.

Voices in the Wilderness

In the heart of the quiet woods,
Voices rise as nature broods.
Echoes of justice, bold and pure,
In the wilderness, we find our cure.

Lost souls wander, searching deep,
Secrets buried that they keep.
In the rustling leaves, a hymn takes flight,
Voices in the wilderness, calling the light.

Mountains linger, ancient and wise,
Through valleys low, their wisdom flies.
In every whisper, a truth confides,
Voices in the wilderness, hope abides.

Beneath the stars that grace the night,
Each heartbeats a longing flight.
In the stillness, a truth we find,
Voices in the wilderness, intertwined.

So listen closely, let your heart hear,
Every challenge brings us near.
In the silence, may we pave a way,
Voices in the wilderness, here to stay.

Soliloquies of the Forsaken

On the edge of sorrow's plight,
Whispers echo through the night.
Forsaken dreams, like ashes fall,
Soliloquies of the forgotten call.

Memories linger, lost in time,
Silent prayers, a quiet rhyme.
Bearing burdens, souls laid bare,
Soliloquies of the forsaken, despair.

Yet in the dark, a flicker glows,
A spark of love that gently knows.
Through the pain, redemption breaks,
Soliloquies of the forsaken, hope awakes.

With every heartbeat, story penned,
A journey longing for the end.
Each voice matters, a tale to share,
Soliloquies of the forsaken, we care.

So lift your gaze, oh heart so worn,
In the dawn, new strength is born.
Together we'll rise from the ache,
Soliloquies of the forsaken, we awake.

Remnants of a Shared Blessing

In the fabric of time, threads entwine,
Remnants linger, a gift divine.
Echoes of laughter, shadows of past,
Remnants of a shared blessing, love's cast.

Gathered hearts in the dance of fate,
Together we stand, it's never too late.
In every trial, a lesson learned,
Remnants of a shared blessing, brightly burned.

Through storm and calm, we find our way,
Gratitude grows with each passing day.
In unity's arms, our spirits rise,
Remnants of a shared blessing, the soul's prize.

So hold the light, let kindness show,
In every corner, we let love flow.
In moments tender, we find our grace,
Remnants of a shared blessing, embrace.

With each embrace, we weave anew,
In the tapestry of life, true.
Together we flourish, forever to sing,
Remnants of a shared blessing, joy we bring.

Incense of a Thousand Regrets

In shadows cast by flickering light,
We gather hopes that take to flight.
Each whispered prayer, a fragile thread,
In the silence, where dreams are fed.

The altar crowded with silent sighs,
Fumes of longing that never dies.
With every breath, regret unfolds,
Our souls' tales in incense told.

Beneath the weight of countless days,
We navigate through lost displays.
Hands clasped tight in fervent plea,
Reflecting on what used to be.

Yet through the smoke, a glimmer gleams,
A hope that thrives in hidden dreams.
For every regret, a chance to mend,
In the heart's journey, we ascend.

So let the incense rise and swirl,
Awakening the sacred pearl.
In the fragrance of our plight,
We discover paths to new light.

Heartbeats in Sacred Time

In the temple where silence speaks,
The heart ignites, and softly seeks.
Each heartbeat echoes through the halls,
A sacred rhythm, where love calls.

Moments unfold like petals wide,
In every pulse, the grace we bide.
Time suspends in a hallowed space,
Where we find the Divine's embrace.

Every breath a gift bestowed,
In the warmth of the sacred road.
The ticking clock, a gentle guide,
In the spirit's dance, we abide.

As shadows lengthen, spirits soar,
We cherish each beat, longing for more.
In the essence of the now we find,
The unity of soul and divine.

So let our heartbeats intertwine,
In sacred time, our souls align.
Together, we weave a tapestry bright,
In the embrace of eternal light.

The Divine Distance of Memory

In the stillness of forgotten years,
Memories linger, warmed by tears.
Each moment a whisper from the past,
In the heart's chamber, forever cast.

We walk the paths of distant grace,
Seeking blessings in time and space.
Footsteps echo on sacred ground,
In the silence, truth is found.

The tapestry of life we thread,
In colors of love, both bright and red.
Each strand a memory, woven tight,
In the heart's embrace, we find our light.

Though distance may veil the eyes,
In the mind's gaze, the spirit flies.
Every heartbeat ties us so,
To the joys and the tears we sow.

So let memory shine, a guiding star,
No matter how near or how far.
In the Divine Distance, we will see,
The beauty of our shared memory.

Keepers of the Unspoken Faith

In the shadows of our quiet prayer,
We gather hopes, a weight we bear.
Each whisper held, a sacred creed,
In the silence, we plant the seed.

The flames flicker, casting shadows tall,
In the heart of night, we heed the call.
Beneath the stars, our spirits rise,
In the stillness, our faith applies.

For every tear that softly falls,
Becomes a hymn in hallowed halls.
Keepers of truth, we stand in grace,
In the unseen, we find our place.

With hands uplifted to the vast unknown,
In the unspoken, seeds are sown.
Together we weave a tapestry bright,
In the embrace of the sacred light.

So let our faith be strong and pure,
In the silence, our hearts endure.
As keepers of the stories we share,
We forge a bond in the sacred air.

Beneath the Broken Sky

Underneath the broken sky,
We search for dreams on high.
Whispers echo through the night,
Guiding souls toward the light.

In shadows deep, we toil and strive,
To find the spark that keeps alive.
Each tear a prayer, each sigh a plea,
For hope to flourish and to be free.

The stars above seem out of reach,
Yet silent lessons they can teach.
In every loss, a chance to grow,
In every heart, the seeds we sow.

Beneath the weight of fallen grace,
We seek the warmth of love's embrace.
Together we shall rise and mend,
Our spirits strong, on faith depend.

So let us walk with heads held high,
Beneath the vast and broken sky.
For in this journey, hand in hand,
We find our truth, we take a stand.

The Prophet of Our Parting

The prophet speaks in quiet tones,
Of love that's lost, and hearts of stone.
He guides our paths with gentle hands,
As we walk through forsaken lands.

Words of wisdom, softly sung,
In every heart, the truth is sprung.
He tells of hope amidst despair,
A light within, beyond compare.

When parting comes, we bow our heads,
In memories deep, the spirit treads.
For every farewell, a seed is sown,
In sacred soil, where love has grown.

Though distances may stretch and bend,
The bond of souls shall not rescind.
In quiet moments, we will see,
The prophet's love will set us free.

So as we part, let hearts unite,
In the darkness, we become light.
The journey calls, we must be brave,
With faith as our eternal wave.

Testament of Fractured Dreams

In shattered realms where shadows creep,
We carry dreams that softly weep.
Each broken fragment tells a tale,
Of hopes that fought but seemed to fail.

Yet in the cracks, the light breaks through,
A testament to what is true.
For every scar that marks the soul,
A story lives, a heart made whole.

Through trials faced, we learn to stand,
With open hearts, we join our hands.
Together we walk this sacred way,
Transcending night to greet the day.

We gather faith in fragile husks,
Resilient souls amidst the rust.
Each breath we take, a prayer released,
In fractured dreams, our hope increased.

So let us write our testament,
In every joy, in every lament.
For in the trials, we shall see,
The beauty in our unity.

Pilgrims of the Heart's Twilight

In twilight's glow, we walk as one,
Pilgrims under the fading sun.
With every step, a prayer we weave,
In the stillness, we learn to believe.

Through winding paths of joy and pain,
We seek the truth that shall remain.
In whispered winds, the spirits call,
To lift us high when shadows fall.

Together we tread the earth so blessed,
With open hearts, we find our rest.
In every heartbeat, there's a song,
That binds us close, where we belong.

Though darkness looms and doubts arise,
The light within shall never die.
With souls ablaze, we chase the dawn,
As pilgrims of the heart, we've drawn.

So let us journey, hand in hand,
Through twilight's grace, we make our stand.
In faith we rise, in love we trust,
Together, forge a path of dust.

The Chime of Forgotten Bells

In silence deep, the echoes fade,
Once vibrant calls, now soft, betrayed.
The towers stand, but voices wane,
As time erodes the sacred strain.

A whisper calls from shadows past,
Where prayers linger, shadows cast.
Hearts once stirred by chimes of grace,
Now wander lost, in empty space.

Yet hope remains within the hearts,
A glimmer shines, though light departs.
For in the stillness, truth shall rise,
Awakening, beneath the skies.

The bells may sleep, but dreams will soar,
Through hallowed halls, forevermore.
And if we listen, we shall hear,
The chime of faith that draws us near.

So let us tread on sacred ground,
Where love and spirit still are found.
In every chime, a truth revealed,
A promise made, a heart congealed.

In the Ruins of Us

We stumbled through, amidst the stone,
In whispered prayers, we faced alone.
The temples crumbled, dreams decayed,
Yet in the rubble, hope displayed.

Each fragment speaks of life's embrace,
In shattered grace, we find our place.
With hands entwined, we bear the weight,
Of yesterdays that shaped our fate.

Though shadows loom, and doubts descend,
Our spirits rise, they will not bend.
For in this grief, a seed shall grow,
Through every pain, a truth to know.

The ruins whisper tales of old,
Of faith and love, and hearts of gold.
We walk the path, though scars remain,
In every loss, a sweet refrain.

So let us build from what is lost,
With love as guide, regardless cost.
In ruins found, our souls unite,
In sacred bond, we still take flight.

A Lament for Lost Sanctity

In quiet tear, our hearts lament,
The sacred vows, so quickly spent.
With every breath, the shadows creep,
A haunting song that stirs our sleep.

For once we danced in light divine,
In harmony, our souls entwined.
But echoes now of what was pure,
Remind us how we must endure.

The altar stands, though faith is thin,
A testament to where we've been.
We seek the flame, though winds may blow,
Through trials faced, our spirits grow.

Yet in this grief, a strength is found,
In love's embrace, we stand our ground.
The light shall pierce the darkest night,
Reclaiming all that is our right.

So let us rise from ashes bare,
Awakened hearts shall mend and care.
For in the mourning, hope will start,
A restoration of the heart.

The Dust of Holy Footprints

Upon this earth, where footsteps tread,
The dust remains, the heart has bled.
In every grain, a story lies,
Of journeys met with hopeful sighs.

The sacred path, we walk anew,
With every step, a chance to view.
The wisdom shared, the love we seek,
In mortal bonds, we find the meek.

For in the dust, the sacred glows,
Each footprint left, a testament shows.
Of battles fought and victories won,
The journey deepens, never done.

Let us embrace the sacred dust,
In every trial, embrace the trust.
With open hearts, we move ahead,
In paths of faith, our spirits fed.

And as we walk where saints have been,
The holy marks, we shall redeem.
In dust and love, together rise,
Awakening beneath the skies.

Beneath the Weight of Ashes

Beneath the weight of ashes fall,
The whispers of the saints call.
In quiet faith, we seek the light,
To guide us through the endless night.

With heavy hearts, we kneel and pray,
For hope to rise, to find our way.
In stillness, find the grace within,
To heal the wounds, to let love win.

Through darkened skies, the stars do gleam,
A flicker of a sacred dream.
In the silence, His voice we hear,
A promise held, forever near.

As shadows dance on hollow ground,
The sacred echoes all around.
We bear our sins, but not alone,
In every heart, a path is sown.

Awake, O spirit, rise and soar,
From ashes, we are evermore.
With reverent breath, the world we face,
Together bound, by love's embrace.

The Last Communion

In twilight's glow, the table set,
The bread of life, we won't forget.
With humble hearts, we gather near,
In love's embrace, we cast out fear.

Each cup we raise, a solemn vow,
To cherish grace – we take it now.
In every sip, a sacred bond,
With open hearts, our spirits respond.

The candles flicker, shadows play,
As voices lift in sweet array.
We feast on mercy, hope, and peace,
In this communion, we find release.

Through trials faced, we've learned to trust,
In every trial, our faith is just.
Together here, in spirit strong,
We sing our praises, the heart's song.

As night descends, the love remains,
In whispered prayers, in joy and pains.
The last communion, a promise shared,
In every heart, a truth declared.

Reverence in Absence

In silence deep, we find our way,
In absence felt, we learn to stay.
With every breath, the memories flow,
In quiet reverence, our spirits grow.

Though loved ones part, their echoes stay,
In sacred moments, night and day.
We hold them close, beyond the veil,
In whispers soft, our hearts set sail.

The stars above, a guiding light,
Through darkest hours, they burn so bright.
In every tear, a story revealed,
In every wound, a truth unsealed.

With tender hearts, we seek to mend,
In absence known, we trust and tend.
As time moves on, the bond remains,
In gentle grace, our love sustains.

Though bodies fade, the spirit sings,
In every loss, the joy it brings.
Reverence pure, in absence cast,
A timeless love that ever lasts.

Hymns of Unheld Hands

In every heart, a hymn resides,
A melody where hope abides.
Though hands unheld may feel alone,
In whispered prayers, our spirits grown.

With every breath, a sacred song,
In unity, we all belong.
In solitude, we find our grace,
A shining light in love's embrace.

The world may turn, but faith persists,
In quiet moments, joy consists.
With hearts entwined, we seek the light,
Our spirits soaring, taking flight.

Though paths diverge, we carry on,
In distant places, love's not gone.
For every tear, a laughter's spark,
In shadows cast, we leave our mark.

So let the hymns of souls combined,
Resound in hearts, forever twined.
In unheld hands, we find our way,
Together still, come what may.

Ascension of the Unseen Heart

In silence, the heart takes flight,
Above the stars, on wings of light.
A whisper calls from realms unknown,
To depths divine, we've gently grown.

Through trials faced beneath the sun,
The unseen path has just begun.
With faith as anchor, strong and true,
The heart ascends, as skies turn blue.

From shadows deep, to heights we soar,
In sacred union, we seek more.
A journey forged in love's embrace,
In every step, we find our grace.

The soul once bound is now set free,
In sacredness, we come to be.
Each heartbeat echoes heaven's song,
In the divine, we all belong.

So let the unseen heart arise,
With every hope that never dies.
In faith, we rise, in trust, we stand,
Together bound, in spirit's hand.

Communion of the Longing Spirit

In twilight's glow, the spirits meet,
With gentle whispers, pure and sweet.
A longing felt, a call to prayer,
In every heart, we find our share.

The sacred bond that joins us all,
In love's embrace, we rise and fall.
Through trials faced, we find our way,
In unity, we learn to sway.

Each yearning breath becomes a hymn,
In stillness deep, we seek within.
A dance of souls beneath the stars,
In longing's light, we heal the scars.

As fragile dreams take flight anew,
In faith, we find the strength we drew.
Through love's communion, hearts entwine,
The spirit longs, and so, we shine.

With open arms, we greet the dawn,
In every moment, we press on.
Together, let our voices soar,
In longing's grace, forevermore.

Chasing Shadows of Reverence

In shadows cast, we seek the light,
With reverence, our spirits bright.
Each moment spent in quiet prayer,
In whispers soft, we feel the air.

Through hills and valleys, we explore,
Chasing shadows, forevermore.
A sacred dance, both fierce and rare,
In faith, we find the strength to care.

The heart ignites with every beat,
In gratitude, we find our seat.
With every trial, each tear we shed,
In reverence, our spirit's fed.

Through storms that gather, fierce and bold,
We chase the light, our stories told.
In every breath, a prayer takes form,
In shadows deep, we seek the warm.

With open hands, we greet the morn,
In every loss, new love is born.
Together, let our spirits rise,
In chasing shadows, seek the skies.

The Celestial Divide

Between the worlds, we draw the line,
In celestial grace, the stars align.
Each heartbeat echoes from above,
In quietude, we find our love.

The heavens whisper, soft and clear,
In holy moments, we draw near.
With open hearts, the veil we part,
To feel the pulse of sacred art.

In twilight shades, the truth unfolds,
A story written, yet untold.
In every journey, light and dark,
We find our way, a holy spark.

The divine breathes through all we seek,
In silence deep, we learn to speak.
Each moment shared, a gift divine,
In unity, our souls entwine.

So let us stand, though worlds collide,
With faith as guide, our hearts abide.
In every step, the love we share,
Fulfills the void, transcends despair.

Reflections in the Water of Time

In the stillness of the night,
Ripples dance, a sacred sight.
Every droplet holds a prayer,
Echoes of our love and care.

Wisdom whispers from the stream,
Life unfolds like a gentle dream.
Past and future intertwine,
In the depths, the spirit shines.

Moonlight paints a silver cross,
In the water, we find the loss.
Yet in sorrow, grace is found,
In every wave, the heart is bound.

Time will pass, yet we remain,
Each reflection, joy and pain.
Let the currents guide our way,
To brighter shores, a new dawn's ray.

In each ripple, trust takes flight,
Through the darkness, find the light.
Hand in hand, we journey forth,
In the water, we seek our worth.

Whispers of Empty Hearts

In shadows deep, where silence dwells,
The heart's soft cry, a sacred spell.
Loneliness, a gentle friend,
In solitude, beginnings blend.

Lost in thoughts that wander far,
Seeking solace in the star.
Chasing echoes of the soul,
Yearning for what makes us whole.

Yet in emptiness, we find grace,
A quiet strength in every space.
Hearts may ache, but love remains,
In whispered prayers, peace sustains.

With every sigh, a tear is shed,
In longing's wake, the spirit's led.
Through barren lands, the heart may roam,
In silence, we are never alone.

Let us cherish the stillness found,
In empty hearts, hope is profound.
For in whispers, we learn to share,
A sacred bond beyond compare.

A Pilgrimage of Solitude

On a winding path, I tread alone,
Each step a prayer, each breath a tone.
Mountains high and valleys low,
In solitude, my spirit grows.

Nature's hymn, a tranquil guide,
In quiet spaces, grace abides.
With every sunrise, burdens fade,
In the silence, faith is laid.

A pilgrimage to valleys deep,
Where thoughts like rivers freely seep.
In every shadow, light is near,
Solitude whispers, 'You are here.'

Wandering through the sacred wood,
In clearings bright, I feel the good.
Each moment, a lesson in peace,
In loneliness, my soul finds release.

So onward I journey, heart in hand,
In stillness, the spirit makes its stand.
For every step upon this way,
Is a dance of love, come what may.

Echoes in the Silent Chapel

In solemn halls where shadows play,
Whispers linger, hearts at bay.
Each echo tells a tale of old,
In the silence, faith unfolds.

Candles flicker, a sacred light,
In the chapel, prayers take flight.
Voices soft, in reverence blend,
In the stillness, we can mend.

Wooden pews, a sacred space,
Where souls meet to seek His grace.
In every corner, hope resides,
In stillness, our spirit guides.

The altar shines, a beacon bright,
In darkness, brings forth the light.
Bowing heads in humble prayer,
In this moment, we are bare.

So let us gather, hearts aligned,
In silent chapel, love confined.
For every echo softly heard,
Is a promise in each word.

Pilgrims on Separate Paths

In the quiet dawn, we tread our way,
With faith as our lantern, we seek the day.
Footprints on soil, where shadows fall,
United in spirit, though apart we call.

River of time flows, carrying our dreams,
Winding through valleys, whispering themes.
Each turn reveals tales of joy and strife,
In the embrace of the journey, we find our life.

Mountains of doubt loom, steep and high,
Yet we climb with courage, reaching the sky.
Hands grasp the promise of hope anew,
For every step taken brings us closer to you.

Winds of change blow, yet we hold the line,
With hearts intertwined, our paths align.
Though miles may divide, our souls remain,
In the temple of love, we'll meet again.

So let us walk forth, though journeys vary,
For every moment, our spirits carry.
In the tapestry woven by the Divine,
Pilgrims we are, forever we shine.

The Solstice of Longing Hearts

In the still of the night, a whisper resounds,
Yearning for peace where love abounds.
Stars twinkle softly, a guide from the skies,
Illuminating dreams that rise and rise.

Hands clasped in prayer, we seek the light,
Hope shines through darkness, banishing fright.
In the solstice hour, our hearts intercede,
For love unending, a sacred creed.

In the embrace of silence, we hear the call,
Echoes of longing, transcending all.
With each tender glance, our spirits mend,
The warmth of connection, a heavenly blend.

Time weaves the fabric of destiny's thread,
Binding our souls, where angels have tread.
The solstice beckons, a night full of grace,
In the dance of the cosmos, we find our place.

So let each heartbeat be a song of love,
Carried by prayers to the heavens above.
In this season of solace, we'll never part,
For one light remains in each longing heart.

The Sacred Weight of Goodbyes

In the twilight glow, shadows begin to creep,
A moment of silence, where memories seep.
Tears like raindrops, fall on the ground,
In the sacred weight, grief is profound.

Hearts once entwined, now tenderly ache,
With whispered farewells, every breath we take.
Love lingers softly, a fragrance so sweet,
In the echo of laughter, our souls meet.

Pages of stories forever unfold,
Each goodbye a lesson, in courage and bold.
Embrace the sorrow, let healing commence,
In the depth of the parting, we find recompense.

Memories, like jewels, sparkle in mind,
Treasured reminders of love intertwined.
As the dawn breaks, new paths will arise,
In the sacred weight, hope never dies.

For every ending, a beginning anew,
In the tapestry woven, the threads are true.
The sacred weight of goodbyes we bear,
In every heartbeat, love lingers there.

Memento Mori in the Chapel of Love

In the chapel's hush, a candle's soft glow,
Whispers of time in the shadows that flow.
Memento mori, the lessons of fate,
In each fleeting moment, we contemplate.

Love's gentle presence, a timeless embrace,
Reminds us of beauty, the strength of grace.
As seasons do turn, so too must we learn,
In the heart of the chapel, the flame shall burn.

Life's fragile dance, a delicate thread,
Interwoven with love, on which we are led.
In the face of farewell, we gather the light,
To cherish each heartbeat, to hold what feels right.

So let not the shadows overshadow the day,
In the chapel of love, we choose to stay.
Embracing the lessons that the ages impart,
Memento mori, live fully, with heart.

In the final embrace, when our journey is done,
We rise like the dawn, with the strength of the sun.
In each echo of memory, we find our refrain,
In the chapel of love, forever remain.

Where the Light No Longer Dwells

In shadows deep where silence reigns,
The whispers fade, the heart now pains.
We seek the glow of grace once near,
But find instead our darkest fears.

The path once bright, a distant lore,
We wander lost from heaven's door.
Each step we take, the echoes call,
Yet none respond; we feel the fall.

In twilight's grip, the soul is bound,
A grasping grasp of sacred ground.
But every prayer seems void of sound,
As hope retreats, thus we are drowned.

Yet in the void where shadows writhe,
A flicker stirs; we learn to strive.
We raise our hands to claim the light,
For faith ignites the endless night.

Through shattered dreams and heavy hearts,
We forge ahead, for grace imparts.
In every tear, a lesson sewn,
We find the strength we thought was gone.

Shattered Prayers and Hollow Hymns

In sacred spaces, echoes fade,
Our hollow hymns, in silence laid.
Prayers once fervent now lie still,
In broken whispers, void of will.

The altar stands, a ghostly sight,
Where faith was strong, now veers from light.
Each trembling voice, a muted sound,
As fractured souls seek holy ground.

Yet still we come, though hearts may ache,
To mend the wounds that time can make.
In shadows thick, we lay our plight,
And seek the balm to heal our night.

For every tear, a prayer does rise,
From depths of sorrow, to the skies.
In every note, a heart yearns still,
To find the peace we long to fill.

And though our hymns may wane and break,
A flicker sparks; we dare to wake.
In shattered prayers, hope reclaims,
The light within, through love's own flames.

The Altar of Our Departure

At twilight's door, we gather near,
With heavy hearts, we shed our fear.
The altar bare, a solemn sight,
We pause to mourn the fading light.

In parting ways, we find our grace,
As fleeting moments we embrace.
Each whispered name, a tender thread,
Connecting lives, though some lie dead.

In memories vast, the echoes swell,
Tales woven deep, we know too well.
Each heart's a page, a sacred tome,
In every sorrow, we find our home.

Yet as we stand, in silence deep,
We gather strength from seeds we keep.
For every ending leads to start,
In love's sweet bloom, we play our part.

In sacred fire, our spirits soar,
We leave behind, yet seek for more.
At every turn, in light we tread,
Embracing all that lies ahead.

Beneath the Veil of Memory

In whispered dreams, the past unfolds,
Beneath the veil, the heart retolds.
Each moment wrapped in tender grace,
Where love once dwelt, time can't erase.

The echoes linger, soft and deep,
In fields of thought where spirits sleep.
We wander through the sacred space,
And find our solace in embrace.

Through joy and sorrow, hand in hand,
We trace the lines, we understand.
For every tear, a smile may rise,
In memories stitched beneath the skies.

With faith we build, though storms may rise,
A tapestry of endless ties.
In every glance, a story found,
Where love and loss together sound.

So let us cherish what we hold,
As time unfolds its quiet fold.
Beneath the veil, forever stay,
In sacred bond, we find our way.

Celestial Tear-Stains on the Altar

In the stillness of the night,
Whispers rise with gentle grace.
Tear-stains brushed on sacred stone,
Hearts uplifted in this space.

Angels weep, their love bestowed,
As prayers weave through the air.
In every drop, a story told,
Of hope and mercy laid bare.

Beneath the glow of heaven's light,
Faithful gather, spirits soar.
Unity through the darkest fight,
Seeking truth forevermore.

In the shadows, burdens shared,
Among the faithful, we cry.
Each sorrow gently repaired,
With love that never says goodbye.

Celestial, the tear-stains glimmer,
A reflection of divine care.
In every heart, a faithful shimmer,
A promise held in silent prayer.

The Last Sermon of Us

In a world where silence reigns,
We gathered 'neath the faded light.
Words of wisdom dimmed by pain,
Yet hearts ignited in the night.

With fervor, we spoke of grace,
In the absence of despair.
Each sorrow carved upon our face,
A testament we laid bare.

From the depths of weary souls,
Resilient spirits intertwine.
Against the tide, our message rolls,
Love transcends the hands of time.

A final sermon softly sung,
Of hope in every soul we find.
In unity, our voices rung,
An everlasting bond defined.

As echoes fade into the night,
We part with hearts forever blessed.
A sacred flame, a guiding light,
In each other, we find rest.

Loneliness Beneath the Starlit Dome

Underneath the vast expanse,
Stars bear witness to our plight.
Drifting souls in quiet trance,
Seeking solace in the light.

Whispers carried on the breeze,
Hearts adrift in endless roam.
Yet within the silence, peace,
Loneliness finds its true home.

Each twinkle tells a story old,
Of love lost and hope regained.
In the dark, we feel the cold,
Yet warmth blooms through faith unchained.

Beneath this dome of endless night,
We search for answers in the stars.
In every tear, a wish takes flight,
Mapping dreams of who we are.

Loneliness, a fleeting guest,
Teaches strength within the void.
In the stillness, we are blessed,
Our spirits intertwined, deployed.

Between Two Worlds Unseen

Between the realms, our spirits dance,
A bridge of faith where shadows play.
In silence held, we take a chance,
To leave our doubts and fears at bay.

The veil is thin, the air divine,
As echoes of the past resound.
Holding hands, our lives entwine,
In the sacred space we've found.

Time stands still in holy grace,
As visions blur with every breath.
Between two worlds, we trace our place,
A promise born from life and death.

With every prayer, a bit of light,
Illuminating paths ahead.
In shared belief, we unite,
With love igniting what we've said.

Silent guardians watch above,
In every step, they lend us wings.
In this unity, we feel love,
And hear the song eternity sings.

Seraphim Weep in Solitude

In shadows deep, the seraphim sigh,
Their wings unfold, beneath the gray sky.
Once clad in light, now veils of despair,
They mourn for souls, lost in the air.

Forgotten hymns on trembling lips fall,
Echoes of love that no longer call.
With tears like rain upon the earth's face,
They weep for all in their silent grace.

Each droplet a prayer, a plea for the lost,
In the stillness they find, redemption's cost.
As time weaves on, in celestial flight,
They long for peace, in the infinite night.

Amidst the stars, their sadness is bright,
A beacon of hope in the divine light.
Seraphim weep, yet their hearts still burn,
For every soul, in the world's cruel turn.

And though they wander in sorrow's embrace,
Their love transcends, defying all space.
In solitude they stand, as ages pass,
Guardians of dreams — their vigil steadfast.

The Unholy Garden of Remembrance

In shadows cast, where silence thrives,
A garden grows, where darkness dives.
Once fertile ground, now treacherous bloom,
The whispers of sin mingle with doom.

Beneath the boughs of the twisted tree,
Souls wander lost, yearning to be free.
Each petal dark holds a story untold,
Of love's betrayal and hearts grown cold.

Ghostly figures in the moonlight dwell,
Bound by the past, in their silent cell.
With roots of regret that intertwine,
Harvesting anguish, a bitter vine.

And yet in the gloom, a flicker of light,
A memory's grace breaks the endless night.
For even the thorns, sharp as they seem,
Can cradle the lost in a fractured dream.

In this unholy ground, shadows entwine,
The sacred and cursed in design.
Yet hope may sprout through cracks in the earth,
Turning sorrow's garden to moments of mirth.

Covenant of the Forgotten

In forgotten realms, where shadows conspire,
A covenant binds hearts with sacred fire.
Souls once cherished, now lost in the night,
Awaiting the dawn to restore their sight.

Promises made under the ancient trees,
In whispers carried by the gentle breeze.
Forgotten dreams linger in twilight's breath,
A testament written in the face of death.

Yet hope revitalizes the fragile bond,
Like rivers of grace that stretch and respond.
Through every tear that has stained the past,
New beginnings bloom, a light ever cast.

In silence, they gather, the weary and worn,
In the embrace of love, the lost are reborn.
A circle of faith, a circle of grace,
Embracing the shadows, finding their place.

Thus, the covenant stands, unbroken and true,
Through the ages it whispers, to me and to you.
For the hearts that are weary and souls that have fought,
Find peace in the battles that time has forgot.

Psalms Written in the Void

In the vastness where silence reigns supreme,
Psalms are penned in a flickering dream.
Carved in stardust, each word shines bright,
Illuminating shadows lost in the night.

For every echo that fades to despair,
A melody of grace drifts through the air.
In the void, where the lonely hearts dwell,
The song of creation begins to swell.

Lines between worlds blur like ancient scrolls,
In whispers of wisdom, it softly consoles.
Though darkness surrounds like a shroud of pain,
Hope arises anew, with every refrain.

Beneath the blanket of celestial night,
Psalms written softly take flight with the light.
In the depths of the void, love's arms endure,
Holding the weary to offer them cure.

So sing to the stars, let your spirit soar,
For in every psalm, there's a door to explore.
In the silence, hear echoes from above,
The psalms of the void, singing endless love.

The Fading Incense

In the temple, shadows dance,
Whispers of prayer, a fleeting chance.
Incense rises, a sacred plea,
Carried by winds, toward Thee.

Hearts once fervent, now hushed and still,
Yearning for grace, seeking Thy will.
Each ember glows with soft despair,
A reminder of love, in silent prayer.

Fingers trace the ancient stone,
In solitude, I am not alone.
The scent of hope fades with the night,
Yet faith persists, a flickering light.

Time drips slowly, like molten gold,
Stories of mercy, a truth retold.
Each drop of incense, a prayer's flight,
A fragrant echo in the twilight.

May I find peace, as embers wane,
In the stillness, seek to sustain.
For in the fading, a promise lies,
In the heart's whispers, love never dies.

Blissful Sorrow

In the valley of tears, we find our grace,
A sacred joy in this weary place.
With every sigh, a hymn we sing,
Embracing loss as a sacred thing.

The weight of sorrow is heavy, yet light,
Each drop of anguish, a guide through the night.
With broken hearts, we gather round,
In the ashes, new hope is found.

Hands held high, we offer our pain,
Each wound a vessel for love's refrain.
In this bittersweet dance, we learn to see,
Through the veil of sorrow, bliss sets us free.

A candle flickers, it casts a glow,
In the depths of despair, we come to know.
That joy and grief walk hand in hand,
Both part of the journey, divinely planned.

With every heartbeat, we rise and fall,
In the echoes of sorrow, we answer the call.
For in the embrace of pain's gentle tether,
We find our strength in the bond we share together.

Between Yesterday and Eternity

In the stillness of dawn, a moment resides,
Where echoes of yesterdays quietly hide.
Between breaths of time, we linger and pause,
Seeking the truth, within the cause.

Waves of the past, they crash and retreat,
Lessons of loss, bittersweet.
Yet in this liminal space, we create,
The threads of our fate, interwoven with grace.

Stars whisper secrets, in the night sky's embrace,
Dancing between moments, finding our place.
As shadows of time stretch toward the light,
We stand on the cusp of day and night.

In the tapestry woven from now and then,
Each heartbeat a prayer, a chance to begin.
Eternity calls in the silence we find,
In the breath of the present, our hearts intertwined.

So let us wander, where time holds no sway,
In each fleeting moment, find the way.
For between yesterday and eternity's grace,
Is where we truly seek our sacred space.

The Veil of Unfulfilled Vows

Behind the veil of whispered dreams,
Lie promises lost in muted streams.
Each vow a thread, pulled tight with care,
Yet some unravel, lost in the air.

In the chapel of hopes, we kneel in prayer,
For the faith we've sown, and the burdens we bear.
Light flickers dim, as shadows grow long,
Each silence a note in a forgotten song.

The heart cradles wishes, unspoken, concealed,
A garden of dreams, often unsealed.
Yet still we linger, in love's embrace,
Hoping to pass through, the veil of grace.

In the tapestry woven, with colors so bright,
Stitches of longing, woven from light.
Each tear that falls, a catalyst sweet,
In the fabric of time, where sorrow and joy meet.

So let us gather, in the stillness of night,
To weave our vows, to rest in the light.
For beyond the veil, where dreams intertwine,
We'll find our way back, to love divine.

Abandoning the Sacred Place

In the echoes of silence I stand,
Once filled with light, now a shadowed land.
The whispers of faith begin to fade,
What once was sacred, now it's betrayed.

I walk through the ruins, a heart full of woe,
Memories linger, but I must let go.
The altar of hope, now covered in dust,
I must find a path, in solitude I trust.

The prayers once spoken, now lost in the air,
Each syllable fading, a heavy despair.
I turn to the heavens, seeking a sign,
To guide my lost spirit, to solace divine.

With every step free, the chains of the past,
The weight of regret no longer held fast.
In search of redemption, I rise from the ashes,
Towards a new dawn, as the old spirit clashes.

Abandoning what was, embracing the new,
A sacred journey with a clearer view.
In the stillness of night, where shadows reside,
I find my true self, no longer to hide.

A Journey Through Emptiness

Through the void I wander, seeking the light,
In the depth of the stillness, I search for insight.
Each step is a choice, in this desolate space,
Where echoes of longing fill up the place.

The absence surrounds me, a blanket of night,
Yet within it, I sense a flicker of sight.
The heartache of distance, a familiar pain,
Leads me to wisdom, through struggle I gain.

I grasp at the shadows, they dance and they play,
But truth is a beacon, it lights up the way.
In this journey of emptiness, I find my soul,
With every step forward, I become more whole.

The lessons of loss, in silence they speak,
From the void I emerge, with spirit unique.
Though lonely the path, it is sacred and pure,
In the depths of the emptiness, I learn to endure.

Each breath a reminder, the void is not fate,
It's a passage to wisdom, a door to create.
So onward I travel, through darkness and night,
A journey of faith towards the ultimate light.

Confessions in the Dark

In the quiet of midnight, my heart lays bare,
Concealed are the secrets that linger with care.
These confessions I whisper to shadows that creep,
Hoping their silence has promised to keep.

The burdens I carry, too heavy to say,
In the darkness, they twist and lead me astray.
Yet here in my stillness, a voice starts to rise,
Revealing my truths beneath the dark skies.

With every confession, a weight starts to lift,
In shadows I ponder the gift of the rift.
The struggles I've hidden begin to unfold,
In the darkness I find what the light has not told.

Each whisper a step towards the dawn of release,
In the depths of the night, I find my own peace.
For the truth, once spoken, carries great might,
Illuminating paths that were lost in the night.

So here I will linger, in silence profound,
For in confessions of darkness, my strength will be found.

The shadows embrace me, I welcome the fight,
For from the abyss, my spirit takes flight.

The Blessing of Unspoken Words

In the stillness between us, a promise resounds,
Unspoken words linger, in silence they're found.
Wrapped in the comfort of moments we share,
There's wisdom in spaces, a sacred affair.

The hush of our hearts, a language divine,
In glances and gestures, our souls intertwine.
Each heartbeat a blessing, though never expressed,
In the quiet communion, our spirits find rest.

What lies in the silence, a treasure untold,
The warmth of connection, more precious than gold.
In the unuttered vows, love's essence is clear,
A powerful presence, forever held near.

Though words may elude us, our hearts understand,
The bond that we cherish, a divine guiding hand.
With every heartbeat, an echo of grace,
The blessing of silence in love's holy space.

So let the unspoken flourish and grow,
In the garden of souls where true feelings flow.
For the blessing of silence is deeper than sound,
In the universe's embrace, our truth can be found.

In the Garden of Remembrance

Beneath the boughs of ancient trees,
Whispers float upon the breeze.
Each petal tells a story true,
Of love that blooms in morning dew.

Time stands still within this space,
Echoes linger, a warm embrace.
In memories where shadows play,
Hearts find peace, and hope will stay.

Each stone a mark of lives once known,
In silent prayer, we sit alone.
The fragrance of the sacred bloom,
Fills the air, dispels the gloom.

As sunlight dances on the ground,
The gentle rustle is a sound.
Of voices carried through the air,
Reminders of our loved ones' care.

In this garden, faith is found,
Roots grow deep in hallowed ground.
Together, we shall remember still,
The bonds of love that ever will.

The Soul's Farewell

In twilight's glow, a spirit soars,
Beyond the stars, through open doors.
Each heartbeat whispers soft and low,
As love transcends the tides of woe.

With every breath, a life unfolds,
In sacred tales that time beholds.
The journey starts where life once ended,
A bridge of grace, eternally mended.

The stars align, a guiding light,
Through darkest hours, a beacon bright.
Their laughter echoes, soft and clear,
As souls embrace what's held so dear.

A final gaze, a tender sigh,
With love, we learn to let them fly.
In every tear, a memory we keep,
A bond that sings, though shadows creep.

As dawn arrives with gentle grace,
We honor them in this sacred space.
The soul's farewell is not the end,
For in our hearts, they still descend.

Grace in the Distance

In quiet hours, grace unfolds,
A story woven, gently told.
The light of dawn, a tender ray,
Guides weary hearts along the way.

Each step we take, a quiet prayer,
With burdens lightened, love to share.
In moments lost and days gone past,
We find our strength, our souls amassed.

Through valleys deep and mountains high,
The spirit stirs, we cannot die.
For grace is present, always near,
In whispered hopes and every tear.

As rivers flow, so love will find,
A pathway through the heart and mind.
With every breath, we draw anew,
To hold the world in grace's view.

So let us walk, hand in hand,
In faith, together we shall stand.
Through trials faced, we will persist,
In grace's arms, we shall exist.

Sacred Echoes of Yesterday

In echoes soft, the past remains,
A melody of joy and pains.
The whispers of the ones before,
Guide restless souls to distant shores.

Each tale inscribed in time's embrace,
Awakens thoughts of love and grace.
In sacred moments, hearts entwine,
Within the fabric, yours and mine.

The lessons carved in ancient stone,
Remind us we are never alone.
In every sunset, every dawn,
A prayer resounds, a bond reborn.

Through trials faced, the spirit learns,
In every loss, a light still burns.
The sacred echoes, strong and clear,
Remind us love continues here.

In quiet nights, we find our way,
With faith to guide, come what may.
So let us walk this path of light,
With sacred echoes, shining bright.

The Eclipsed Light of Promises

In shadows cast by fleeting time,
The promises of light still shine.
They flicker softly, guiding back,
Through darkness' hold, we stay on track.

With faith as armor, hearts held high,
We seek the truth beyond the sky.
In whispered hopes and silent prayer,
We find the strength to venture there.

The dawn will break, the glow will rise,
Each promise kept beneath the skies.
Through trials faced, we journey on,
The light of love will lead us home.

Though nights may fall and shadows creep,
In sacred trust, our souls shall leap.
For every star that fades from sight,
Brings forth the dawn, renewing light.

So let us walk this sacred way,
With hearts aglow and spirits gay.
The eclipsed light will guide our way,
To brighter shores where shadows sway.

Chronicles of What Remains

In whispers soft, the tales are spun,
Of battles fought and valor won.
The chronicles of what remains,
Are etched in hearts, not lost to pains.

Each story holds a sacred flame,
Recalling joy, and sorrow's name.
Through trials faced with steadfast grace,
We find our truth in each embrace.

With every tear, a lesson learned,
In every heart, a light discerned.
The ties of love that never break,
Guide weary souls, our bonds awake.

The echoes of the past still speak,
In sacred moments, strong, not weak.
Together we weave a vibrant tale,
As faith and hope will never fail.

So let us treasure what remains,
In every joy and all the pains.
The chronicles unite our plight,
As we embrace the endless light.

The Sacred Road to Silence

Upon the path where silence breathes,
The sacred road, where spirit weaves.
In stillness found, the heart does soar,
A sacred quest for something more.

With every step, a prayer unfolds,
In solemn whispers, truth is told.
The world may fade, the noise subside,
In sacred silence, love will glide.

Through trials faced, serenity grows,
In gentle peace, our spirit knows.
With humble hearts, we tread this way,
To find the light within our day.

Each moment still, a chance to glean,
The divine grace that lies unseen.
The sacred road leads us to peace,
Where all our burdens find release.

So walk with faith, through silence grand,
With open hearts and lifted hands.
The sacred road, our guiding light,
Will lead us home, to endless night.

Prayers at the Threshold

At the threshold where shadows meet,
We gather close, in prayer discreet.
With every word, our spirits rise,
In hopes and dreams beneath the skies.

With trembling hearts, we seek the way,
In whispered tones, we humbly pray.
The door stands wide, our fears released,
In faith we find our longing cease.

Each prayer a beacon, shining bright,
A guiding star in darkest night.
Together we stand, hand in hand,
With love that spans a sacred land.

In unity, our voices blend,
As time and space begin to mend.
With every breath, the promise grows,
In prayers of peace, our spirit knows.

So let us linger at this place,
With open hearts and warm embrace.
At the threshold, many paths extend,
In prayerful hope, our souls ascend.

Sacred Fragments

In quiet halls where whispers dwell,
The fragments of our prayers do swell.
Echoes of faith in the night air,
Guiding lost souls, a gentle care.

Each shard of hope, a light divine,
Together they form a sacred line.
Hearts entwined, a chorus sings,
In harmony, the spirit springs.

Through trials faced, we find our way,
In darkest nights, we seek the day.
With every breath, we ask for grace,
To find in pain a holy space.

In sacred silence, we unite,
Filling the void with love's pure light.
Though fragments scattered, still we stand,
Together we rise, hand in hand.

So let us cherish what remains,
In brokenness, true love sustains.
For every piece, a story told,
In faith we gather, brave and bold.

A Covenant of Sorrow

Beneath the weight of heavy skies,
In sorrow's breath, the spirit sighs.
We bind our hearts in sacred trust,
A covenant formed from dust to dust.

With tears of grief, we carve our way,
Through valleys deep where shadows play.
Each drop a prayer, each cry a plea,
In the embrace of this mystery.

Should the world forsake its grace,
We find our strength in love's embrace.
Together we tread this winding path,
In moments of joy, in shades of wrath.

Though darkness lingers, hope will rise,
In every heart, a glimpse of skies.
For every sorrow that we bear,
The promise blooms in fervent prayer.

So let us stand, unbroken, true,
In the light of grace, we're born anew.
A covenant forged in struggles met,
Embracing love, with no regret.

Seraphim Weep in Quiet

Above the clouds in heaven's light,
Seraphim gaze through the endless night.
With every tear, a sacred vow,
In silence deep, they bless us now.

Their wings unfurl, a gentle breeze,
Carrying whispers through the trees.
In sacred hush, they softly cry,
For every soul that passes by.

They know the pain of life below,
The trials faced and hearts that grow.
In every wound, a lesson learned,
In every flame, the spirit burned.

For beauty blooms from ashes gray,
In every loss, a brighter day.
So let us feel their tender strain,
In quiet moments, love remains.

As seraphim weep, let us pray,
For strength to carry on our way.
In sacred harmony, unite,
With every tear, we find the light.

The Aftermath of Holy Bonds

In the aftermath of sacred binds,
We seek the peace the spirit finds.
Through trials faced, our hearts align,
In love's embrace, the stars will shine.

The brokenness reveals our depth,
In every heartbeat, love is kept.
We journey on through pain and strife,
For in the dark, we find our life.

Through shattered dreams, the hope remains,
In every loss, the love still reigns.
A testament to what we are,
The bonds we forge, our sacred scar.

So let us rise from ashes wide,
In unity, let faith abide.
For in the aftermath we see,
The strength found in community.

With every breath, renew the vow,
In love's sweet name, we echo now.
Together, we shall stand as one,
In every battle, love has won.

The Ascension of My Heart

In the stillness of the night, I rise,
Wings unfurling to touch the skies.
A whisper beckons my soul to soar,
Guided by love, forevermore.

Each step a prayer upon the breeze,
Dancing shadows of ancient trees.
With every heartbeat, faith ignites,
A journey woven in holy lights.

The stars align, a celestial guide,
With hope and grace, I shall abide.
In the embrace of the divine glow,
I find the strength to let love flow.

As the mountains echo my plea,
In every valley, Your spirit I see.
The song of angels, a sacred art,
Resides forever in my heart.

As the dawn breaks upon the earth,
I breathe in deeply, embraced by mirth.
For in this moment, so pure, so bright,
My heart ascends into the light.

Sacred Echoes in Solitude

In quiet chambers of the soul,
Where whispers dance and shadows roll.
I find the echoes of my prayer,
A balm of silence, divinely rare.

Each thought a lantern, softly glows,
Illuminating the path I chose.
The stillness wraps around me tight,
A sacred refuge, warm and bright.

In solitude, I hear Your call,
The heartbeat of the universe, enthralled.
In every breath, a promise clear,
You dwell within, forever near.

The moments stretch, a timeless grace,
Your presence felt in this holy place.
Together in silence, we find our way,
In the sacred echoes, come what may.

With every sigh, a soul reborn,
From darkness into the light of morn.
In solitude, I learn to see,
The boundless love that sets me free.

Between the Candles and the Silence

In the soft glow of flickering light,
I pause and ponder the endless night.
Between the flames, a story winds,
Of grace and mercy that love finds.

A quiet prayer dances in the air,
As shadows whisper of sacred care.
Each candle burns with purpose true,
A beacon shining, guiding you.

In the stillness, I hear the song,
Of saints and angels, where we belong.
With each flicker, my faith ignites,
In the space between, the spirit heightens.

Between the candles, in silence deep,
I weave my dreams, my soul to keep.
God's gentle touch upon my brow,
A sacred promise, here and now.

So let the candles light the way,
In darkness met with hope's array.
For between the flickers, I find my trust,
In love eternal, both pure and just.

When the Sacrament Turns to Dust

In the twilight of the sacred feast,
Where prayers rise, and spirits cease.
I ponder life when love decays,
And faith is cloaked in shadowed haze.

When the wine spills and bread's grown stark,
I seek the light within the dark.
For every crumb, a memory dear,
Reminds me of grace that draws us near.

Though the body fades, the soul stays bright,
In every loss, there shines a light.
For even dust can dance and sing,
In the moments held by everlasting.

Each sacrifice a tale of grace,
In the silence, I search for face.
When the world dims and hopes combust,
The spirit rises; it's love robust.

So let the sacrament find its way,
Transform the night, embrace the day.
For even in dust, we're never lost,
In love eternal, we pay the cost.

Whispers of a Faded Blessing

In shadows deep where echoes dwell,
The fading light begins to swell.
A prayer lingers in the air,
A gentle whisper, a solemn care.

Hearts entwined in holy grace,
Seeking solace in this place.
With every breath the spirit sighs,
In the stillness, love never dies.

Hope flickers like a candle's flame,
In whispers soft, we call Your name.
Through trials faced, we rise anew,
With faith unbroken, ever true.

The journey winds through dark and light,
With every step, we seek the right.
Each blessing cherished, none too small,
In faded whispers, we heed the call.

For as the dusk gives way to dawn,
In sacred trust, we carry on.
Though blessings fade, they'll find their way,
Through whispered prayers, we choose to stay.

The Sacred Silence Between Us

In quietude, the heart does speak,
In silence shared, we find the meek.
As souls connect without the sound,
In sacred spaces, love is found.

The hush that falls, a gentle night,
A tranquil pause, a soft delight.
In stillness deep, our spirits fly,
With whispered hopes that touch the sky.

Though words may falter, truth remains,
In silence bound, we break our chains.
A bond unseen, yet deeply felt,
In sacred silence, love will melt.

The moments shared, so pure, so rare,
In every glance, a whispered prayer.
As hearts align in timeless grace,
In sacred silence, we embrace.

Together we find solace sweet,
A silent song, our hearts compete.
In depths of quiet, we discover,
The sacred silence pulls us closer.

Pilgrimage of Lost Souls

We wander paths of shadowed dreams,
In search of light, our spirit beams.
With weary feet, we roam the night,
A pilgrimage toward the light.

Each step we take, a story told,
In search of truth, both brave and bold.
Through valleys dark and mountains high,
With faith in hearts, we touch the sky.

Lost souls unite in common quest,
In troubled times, we seek the blessed.
Through trials faced, we learn to cope,
With every journey, we find hope.

The road is long, the weight is vast,
Yet in our hearts, the die is cast.
For every sorrow bears a tale,
In pilgrimage, we shall not fail.

With open arms, we greet the dawn,
A light emerging, fears withdrawn.
In unity, we find our role,
This sacred journey of lost souls.

Echoes of a Sacred Farewell

Upon the altar, memories rest,
In whispered sighs, we feel the blessed.
As shadows dance 'neath twilight skies,
In echoes soft, our spirit flies.

The flames of love burn ever bright,
In sacred glow, we seek the light.
With every tear that gently falls,
We hear the echoes of love's calls.

Though farewells pierce the heart so deep,
In every tear, our promise we keep.
For in the silence that remains,
The echoes of their love sustains.

We gather strength, though time may part,
The sacred bonds unite the heart.
Through every echo, we find peace,
In memories held, our love won't cease.

And as we turn to face the night,
In every star, they share their light.
The echoes linger, never stray,
In sacred farewells, they stay.

Reverie of the Departed

In quiet grace they softly tread,
Beyond the veil where few have led.
Their whispers linger, pure and bright,
Guiding souls through endless night.

A tapestry woven with love's thread,
In sacred moments, memories spread.
The echoes of laughter fill the air,
In every tear, a silent prayer.

Beneath the stars, their spirits soar,
As time reveals what came before.
In dreams, they visit, light the way,
In gentle peace, we find our stay.

With every heartbeat, they abide,
In corners of the heart, they hide.
For love transcends the earthly bound,
In reverie, their grace is found.

So let us honor their sweet rest,
In treasured moments, they are blessed.
For in the stillness, we will see,
In reverie, they live, they free.

A Pilgrim's Heart

Through narrow paths, the pilgrim roams,
With faith as guide, he finds his home.
Each step unfolds the sacred quest,
In trials faced, the spirit's test.

The sun will rise upon his way,
With hope held high in light of day.
In every shadow, a lesson learned,
With every flame, a passion burned.

The dazzling skies, the whispering trees,
Remind him of life's mysteries.
In solitude, he finds the peace,
Where worldly cares begin to cease.

Upon the mountains, vast and wide,
He feels the presence by his side.
In every prayer, a promise made,
In every heartbeat, love displayed.

Among the stars, his dreams take flight,
A pilgrim's heart, a beacon bright.
Through winding roads, he journeys far,
In search of home, to find the star.

Unbound

In realms beyond where spirits dwell,
The chains of earth no longer swell.
With wings of grace, they rise and sing,
In freedom's arms, their voices ring.

The whispered winds, a gentle caress,
Unraveling time, they find their rest.
In every heartbeat, souls collide,
In love's embrace, they now reside.

No bounds to hold, no fears to face,
In endless light, they find their place.
Each journey taken, one with all,
In unity, they rise and fall.

What once was lost, now found anew,
In vibrant hues of every view.
For in this space, the soul expands,
In peace secured by gentle hands.

So let us wander without the weight,
In love's deep realm, we elevate.
For unbound hearts forever soar,
In timeless realms, forevermore.

The Other Side of Solace

In shadows cast by silent tears,
We find the light that calms our fears.
The other side where solace waits,
In tender grace, the spirit integrates.

With whispered dreams that fill the night,
The heart, once heavy, takes to flight.
In tranquil moments, peace unfolds,
And in the quiet, love is told.

Each wound, a pathway to the soul,
In searching depths, we find the whole.
The other side, a tender grace,
In barren fields, we find our place.

Through endless dusk, the dawn will break,
And in that light, our hearts awake.
In golden rays, the hope is bright,
Beyond the veil, we see the light.

So journey forth, dear heart, in trust,
For solace lives, in love, we must.
Let not the dark erase the dawn,
In every tear, a hope reborn.

Divine Absence

In stillness rests the divine abode,
Where silence speaks the truth bestowed.
In absence felt, the heart will yearn,
For in the void, we come to learn.

A gentle touch, a fleeting grace,
In every space, we seek the face.
For though unseen, each breath is felt,
In every ache, the spirit's melt.

Through trials faced, the soul will soar,
In every loss, we gain much more.
The beauty lies in faith beneath,
In divine absence, we find belief.

So let the heart refrain from doubt,
In every whisper, hear the shout.
For in the stillness, love's refrain
In absence dwells, yet still remains.

In every moment, time reveals,
The divine presence that ever heals.
With open hearts, we transcend the strife,
In divine absence, we find our life.

Shadows Beneath the Stained Glass

In the quiet whispers of the eve,
Shadows dance where spirits weave.
Colors cast from heaven's grace,
Bathe the world in a gentle embrace.

Each pane tells stories old and wise,
Of faith that soars, of love that cries.
A flicker of hope in the darkest night,
Guiding souls toward the light.

Here, the weary find their peace,
In prayerful silence, all fears cease.
Each heart a lantern, each tear a star,
Illuminated paths, though journeys are far.

Through archways of sorrow, joy shall stream,
In the sacred stillness, life's vibrant dream.
Let not the shadows claim their own,
For in this sanctuary, love is known.

So linger a while beneath this dome,
Feel the presence; you are not alone.
In every color, in every sound,
Faith and grace eternally abound.

The Prayer of a Wandering Soul

Oh guide me, Lord, through paths unknown,
In every sigh, let Your love be shown.
A heart that seeks, yet feels so lost,
I'll bear my burden, no matter the cost.

Across the hills where shadows lay,
In the stillness of night, I seek Your way.
Words of solace fill the air,
Whispers of mercy, a tender care.

Let my spirit rise on wings of grace,
To find the love in every place.
With each step taken, may I discern,
The fire of faith within me burn.

In the silence, I long to hear,
Echoes of hope that whisper clear.
Guide my footsteps to where You stand,
A weary traveler in Your hand.

So wrap me in Your light divine,
Awake my heart, make Your will mine.
For I am lost, but now I know,
With every prayer, Your love will flow.

Lost in the Sanctuary of Memory

In sacred chambers where silence sleeps,
Memories linger; their promise keeps.
Pillars of faith hold stories near,
Each heart echoes what we hold dear.

Moments etched in the tapestry of time,
Whispering grace in a sacred rhyme.
With every breath, a prayer takes flight,
In this haven of shadows and light.

Let the echoes of laughter resound,
In the hallowed walls, love is found.
Each tear shed, a seed of grace,
Blooms anew in this holy place.

Rekindle the fire of steadfast trust,
In the ashes of sorrow, rise we must.
For every longing, a hymn shall rise,
Lost in the sanctuary, faith never dies.

So gather your thoughts, let the past unfold,
In the arms of memory, we are bold.
In this sacred refuge, we are made whole,
In the sanctuary, we find our soul.

When the Light Fades

When the light fades and shadows creep,
Hold me close in the silence deep.
Where is the flame that once burned bright?
In the darkness, restore my sight.

In the stillness, I seek Your face,
With every heartbeat, grant me grace.
Though moments falter, faith shall rise,
A beacon of hope in weary eyes.

Guide me through valleys of despair,
In the echoes of prayer, hear my care.
Let the dawn break the chains of night,
When the light fades, be my light.

In whispers soft, Your spirit calls,
Through the trials, Your love enthralls.
Though weariness grips, my soul will sing,
For in darkness, Your light will spring.

So grant me strength for the road ahead,
With every tear, my spirit fed.
For when the light fades, I shall find,
In the shadows, Your peace aligned.

Psalms of the Forgotten

In shadows deep, where whispers dwell,
The souls once bright, now fade like shells.
Their cries, a song lost in the night,
Yet still they seek the dawn's soft light.

O spirits bound by chains of time,
Your echoes hum, a sacred rhyme.
With every tear that falls like rain,
We hold your hopes, your silent pain.

From dust to dust, your tales remain,
In heart and mind, your love's refrain.
Though generations may pass by,
In faith and prayer, your flame will fly.

Let us not forget the names once sung,
For in our hearts, they're always young.
With gratitude, we lift our voice,
In unity, we make our choice.

To honor those who came before,
Their wisdom ours, forevermore.
In gratitude, this psalm we raise,
For all the forgotten, we give praise.

The Altar of Longing

At the altar where dreams reside,
We bow our heads, our hearts open wide.
In whispers soft, our hopes ignite,
For love and peace, we seek the light.

Each prayer a journey, a path unknown,
In faith we gather, together, alone.
With every plea, a sacred breath,
We dance with life, we challenge death.

The candles burn with tender grace,
Illuminating each longing face.
In shadows cast, our stories weave,
A tapestry of hearts that grieve.

We yearn for answers, we long for peace,
In this sacred space, our worries cease.
With tears that fall like gentle dew,
We find in silence, our spirits renew.

O altar high, where dreams ascend,
Our brokenness, you seek to mend.
In fervent prayer, we rise above,
In longing hearts, we find our love.

A Testament to What Was

In golden fields where shadows fade,
A testament in silence laid.
The echoes of a life once known,
In whispers soft, their seeds are sown.

Through laughter bright and tears that flow,
In stories shared, the heart can grow.
Each moment cherished, memory cast,
A bridge of time, built strong and vast.

O past, your lessons guide our way,
In every night, the promise of day.
With gratitude, we recall the grace,
In every moment, a sacred space.

We honor journeys, both wide and steep,
In joyful hearts, your whispers keep.
A testament, in love we find,
The threads of life forever bind.

In every leaf that turns to gold,
A story of the brave and bold.
In remembrance, our spirits soar,
For what was lived, we yearn for more.

Silent Devotions

In quiet hours, where stillness reigns,
Our hearts commune in gentle chains.
In breaths so soft, we seek the divine,
With every silence, a sacred sign.

As dawn unfolds in hues of grace,
We find our refuge in this place.
With humble hearts, we bow in prayer,
In silent devotions, love we share.

Each thought a prayer, each sigh a song,
In simple truths, we all belong.
Through trials faced, our faith shines bright,
In silent whispers, we embrace the light.

As night descends, the stars appear,
In cosmic beauty, we draw near.
Each twinkle speaks of hopes and dreams,
In silent devotions, our spirit beams.

So may we gather in hearts aligned,
In silence deep, our souls entwined.
For in this stillness, we shall find,
The quiet power of the mind.

When Faith Meets Heartache

In shadows cast by sorrow's hand,
A heart aches softly, seeking land.
Yet whispers of hope, a gentle breeze,
Guide the soul through trembling trees.

Each tear a prayer, each sigh a song,
In the silence where we all belong.
With faith as a lantern in the dark,
We traverse paths, igniting a spark.

The burden heavy, yet grace remains,
In heartache's throes, love breaks the chains.
Through thorns of doubt, blooms courage pure,
Our spirits rise, steadfast and sure.

Let not despair shroud joy's sweet light,
For dawn creeps softly, ending night.
In trust we stand, in love we fight,
With faith as our armor, shining bright.

So when the world feels cold and bare,
Lift your eyes, breathe in the air.
For every heartache, a tale is spun,
When faith meets heartache, we are one.

The Temple of Memories

In corners where echoes softly dwell,
Whispers of moments, stories to tell.
Each heartbeat a brick, each laugh a beam,
Building a temple from hope's warm dream.

Golden halos cast by the sun,
Reflecting the journeys, each race we've run.
In the stillness, the past comes alive,
A place of solace, where we revive.

Through windows of time, we peer and see,
The love that shaped our destiny.
Every memory a sacred rite,
Illuminated by faith's gentle light.

In this temple, we gather near,
Holding our visions, crystal clear.
Each sorrow, a stepping stone,
In memories sacred, we are never alone.

As we walk through these hallowed halls,
Every laugh and every tear calls.
Together we stand, hearts intertwined,
In this temple of memories, forever enshrined.

Lamentations in the Stillness

In the hush of the night, the spirit weeps,
A heart in shadow, where silence keeps.
With each lament, a story unfolds,
Of battles fought and dreams left cold.

Yet in stillness, the soul takes flight,
Finding solace in the softest light.
With gentle hands, we mend the fray,
Transforming sorrow, come what may.

Voices rise like incense, sweet,
In the quiet, one finds their beat.
Through tear-stained prayers, we seek the divine,
In lamentations, our spirits entwine.

A chorus of hearts, united and strong,
In the stillness, we find where we belong.
For every tear, a river flows,
In mournful grace, the heart knows.

With courage borne from sacred ache,
In every lament, new paths we make.
Embracing the quiet, the heartstrings play,
In the stillness, we find our way.

The Lost Gospel of Us

In pages worn, our tale is scribed,
A lost gospel, where love has thrived.
Each chapter penned with grace and care,
In the book of life, we laid it bare.

Through trials faced and storms endured,
The essence of us, forever assured.
In whispered vows and golden hours,
We built a life adorned with flowers.

Yet shadows fell, and silence grew,
As memories faded, love felt askew.
In the depths of despair, we seek
The words unsaid, the heart to speak.

With faith as our compass, we navigate,
Finding the way to reconnect our fate.
The gospel of us, a truth profound,
In every heartbeat, love can be found.

So let us rise from ashes and dust,
Reclaim the story, rekindle our trust.
Together we write the verses anew,
In the lost gospel of us, forever true.

Sacrament of Silent Goodbyes

In whispers soft, we part our ways,
With heavy hearts, we seek the rays.
Each moment shared, now fades like mist,
In sacred silence, we feel the twist.

Fading echoes of laughter, we hold dear,
In the hollow shadows, we shed a tear.
The grace of time, a gentle thief,
In every farewell, we find belief.

Beneath the stars, our thoughts align,
In prayerful hopes, we seek the divine.
Together apart, we find the light,
In silent goodbyes, we find our might.

Blessed are the souls that drift apart,
With loving kindness etched on the heart.
In every ending, a new beginning,
In the depths of loss, there's still winning.

With every step, we learn to tread,
In the tapestry of life, we're wed.
The sacrament of love does remain,
Even in silence, joy and pain.

Lost in the Labyrinth of Longing

In corridors of memory, I roam,
Seeking the path that leads me home.
Each turn I take, the shadows grow,
In the labyrinth's depths, my heart's aglow.

The whispers of souls lost in the night,
Guide my weary heart toward the light.
With every sigh, a prayer ascends,
In this web of desire, our spirit bends.

Yearning souls entwined in a dance,
In the quiet moments, we take a chance.
Through the maze of dreams, we drift and sway,
In the labyrinthine night, we find our way.

Oh, the ache of what we desire,
In the silence, unquenchable fire.
Even in shadows, the heart can see,
In longing's embrace, we find the key.

To wander is to seek, to see beyond,
In every heartbeat, we feel the bond.
Though lost in the labyrinth of our minds,
The souls of the faithful are often entwined.

Chanting in the Shadow of Defeat

In the stillness, our voices rise,
A chant of hope beneath dark skies.
Shadows linger, but we stand tall,
In defeat's grip, we will not fall.

With heavy hearts, we unite as one,
In the shadowed valleys, under the sun.
Fear may whisper, but faith will shout,
In every struggle, we rise without doubt.

The echoes of trials, we gently embrace,
In the dance of trials, we find our place.
Through the darkness, a beacon shines,
In the song of resilience, our spirit aligns.

Against the odds, we carry on,
In the depths of sorrow, hope is drawn.
As we gather strength from bonds we hold,
In the chant of life, our stories unfold.

With every note, we forge our fate,
In the shadows of defeat, we create.
Together we stand, our voices soar,
In the chant of resilience, forevermore.

The Reverent Dust of What Remains

In the quiet corners where memories dwell,
Lies the essence of stories we long to tell.
The dust gathers softly, a silken shroud,
In reverence we stand, heads softly bowed.

In the ruins of time, we search for grace,
Through the lens of loss, we find our place.
Each fragment of history whispers a prayer,
In the stillness, we know that love's always there.

The reverent dust of what we once knew,
Carries the warmth of the souls we grew.
In every heartbeat, their echoes persist,
In the tapestry of life, they are missed.

Through twilight's embrace, we seek the light,
In the dance of shadows, they guide our flight.
For every end, there's a seed that is sown,
In the soil of memory, we find our own.

With gratitude, we honor the past,
In the reverent dust, our love will last.
In the sacred silence, we hear the call,
Of those who've left, yet still stand tall.

The Exodus of Love

From the land of sorrow, we depart,
Through the desert's embrace, we start.
In the sands of time, our spirits soar,
Guided by light, forevermore.

With faith as our compass, we seek the way,
Hand in hand, we'll never stray.
The pillars of hope, they rise so tall,
In the heart of love, we find our all.

Upon the mountains, voices will sing,
Rejoicing in the freedom love can bring.
Through the trials, we stand as one,
In the glory of the rising sun.

In the silence, prayers are made,
For the broken paths that we have laid.
With each step forward, we cleanse our past,
Finding strength in love, we are steadfast.

So let the journey be our guide,
In the shelter of grace, we will abide.
For love, our refuge, a holy flame,
In the Exodus, we rise, proclaiming His name.

Broken Vows

In the shadow of promises unkept,
Whispers of heartache, silently crept.
Words once sacred now linger in vain,
Echoing softly, a heart's deep pain.

Through the chambers of love, we once rang,
Now the silence, a haunting clang.
Beneath the weight of the dreams we built,
Lies the sorrow of love's sweet guilt.

As the altar of hope begins to fade,
Tears of remorse wear deep the shade.
Yet in the ashes of what we've lost,
We seek redemption, no matter the cost.

In fractured remnants, truth may come,
Heartbeats echo, a forgotten drum.
With every tear that falls to the ground,
A new vow emerges, with love profound.

For in the breaking, we find the light,
In the wounds of love, a chance to rewrite.
With open hearts ready to mend,
We rise from the ashes, anew we ascend.

Healing Light

In the depths of night, where shadows dwell,
A softly glowing presence begins to swell.
Like a gentle whisper caressing the soul,
The healing light makes broken hearts whole.

Through the trials of life, we stumble and fall,
Yet the light of grace answers our call.
With each ray shining, our burdens lift,
Bestowing upon us a sacred gift.

In the warmth of compassion, we find our way,
Guided by love that will never sway.
Through the pain and sorrow, hope takes flight,
Transforming darkness into brilliant light.

With every step on this sacred ground,
In the arms of the divine, peace is found.
Healing our hearts, love's gentle embrace,
In the journey of life, we discover grace.

Together we stand, in the circle of trust,
Embracing the light, as we know we must.
For in every tear, a lesson is shown,
In the healing light, we are never alone.

When Stars Refuse to Shine

In the canvas of night, where dark clouds loom,
A silence falls heavy, foreboding gloom.
When the stars refuse to light the sky,
Whispers of hope plead, and we sigh.

In the moments of doubt, in shadows we stray,
Yet faith like a beacon may guide our way.
For even in darkness, love's embers remain,
Waiting to burst forth through sorrow and pain.

With hearts entwined, we gather as one,
Trusting the dawn will emerge with the sun.
In the stillness, we search for the spark,
Believing in light, even in the dark.

Each heartbeat a promise, more precious than gold,
In prayers for strength, a story unfolds.
Though stars may be hidden, their shine is still there,
Guiding our spirits through heartache and care.

So let your heart sing when the dark clouds surround,
For the brilliance of love will always be found.
In the tapestry woven by heaven's own hand,
When stars refuse to shine, united we stand.

The Mourning of Lost Prayers

In the garden of longing, where silence grips tight,
The prayers of the faithful dissolve into night.
Each whisper a heartbeat, a soft, tender sigh,
In the mourning of lost dreams, we question the sky.

With hands raised in hope, the heavens we crave,
Yet the echoes of longing bring shadows so grave.
In the stillness of night, our souls start to weep,
For the prayers left unheard, in the silence so deep.

Yet in this mourning, a fire may ignite,
As hearts turn to yearning, they seek for the light.
In each tear that falls, a seed is then sown,
To reveal the beauty that blooms from our own.

In the depths of despair, our spirits may sigh,
But the love that surrounds us will never say die.
For even lost prayers can weave a new way,
Transforming our sorrow to joy in the day.

So we mourn not in vain, but in longing for peace,
For the whispers of love will bring sweet release.
In the heart of our grief, we find what we seek,
Healing the wounds in the prayers that we speak.

Milton Keynes UK
Ingram Content Group UK Ltd.
UKHW020040271124
451585UK00012B/956

9 789916 897829